Paleo Chicken Step-by-Step Make, Healthy Chicken Recipes

Delicious, Healthy, and Easy-to-Make Paleo Chicken Recipes

Chef Paolo Ferrari

Copyright © 2015 by Chef Paolo Ferrari

Introduction:

The Paleo diet is the healthiest plan in the world, requiring no starvation, and no horrendous, continuous exercise. It looks to the ways in which our ancestors ate, all those thousands of years before, when things like diabetes, obesity, and heart disease did NOT rule the earth—as they do today. And, with that past diet plan, we discover: a healthier way to lose weight, to prevent diseases, and to ward off serious mental issues, like depression and anxiety.

The Paleo diet offers an essential weight loss and healthy lifestyle plan. The diet plan works with the way your body has evolutionarily evolved to give you the food you naturally crave—the food that will help you age well, live well, and drop pounds from your waistline.

Chicken is the perfect ingredient in this Paleo diet recipe book, offered here over forty times to bring bountiful proteins, fats, and minimal carbohydrates for a perfect weight loss plan.

Chicken has an extraordinary amount of tryptophan, which is a comforting amino acid that refutes depression and boosts your serotonin levels. Therefore, eating chicken actually makes you happier—which is very important during the winter months, when grey skies and general poor diets make us all feel a little blue.

Furthermore, chicken is important as you age, because it actually prevents bone loss. Thusly, it can refute your chances for arthritis and osteoporosis.

Because the Paleo diet works well with your body, giving you what you need to live well, to lose weight, and to feel fully satisfied, this book is an essential element on your way to bettering yourself.

Good luck preparing these easy, step-by-step paleo chicken recipes. Learn to better yourself, one delicious meal at a time.

Table of Contents

Introduction: 2

Table of Contents 4

Chapter 1. Paleo Chicken Salad Recipes 6
   Thai-Inspired Bok Choy Chicken Salad 6
   From the Garden Basil Chicken Salad 9
   Chinese-Based Cabbage Chicken Salad 10
   Mexican-Inspired Chicken Taco Salad 12
   Indian-Inspired Paleo Curry Chicken Salad 14
   Cilantro and Lime Tangy Chicken Salad 16
   Brussels Sprouts-Based Chicken Salad 17
   Avocado-Based Paleo Chicken Salad 19
   Paleo Inspiration Apple and Chicken Hash Salad 20

Chapter 2. Paleo Chicken Soup, Chili, and Stew Recipes. 22
   Paleo Lazy Day Chicken Veggie Soup 22
   Kale Creation Chicken Soup 24
   Paleo Texas-Living Chicken Tortilla Soup 26
   Thai-Inspired Pumpkin and Chicken Soup 28
   Faux Chicken Noodle Soup 30
   Chicken Sausage Farm Days Soup 32
   Paleo White Winter Wonderland Chicken Chili 34
   Delicious Chipotle Chicken Chili 36
   Mexican-Inspired Chicken Chili 38
   Paleo Faux-Cream Southern Living Chicken Stew 40
   Mediterranean Chicken Stew 42
   African-Inspired Chicken Stew 44

Chapter 3. Paleo Chicken Just-for-Kids Recipes 46
   Thai-Inspired Kid-Friendly Paleo Chicken Pizza 46
   Finger Lickin' Good Kid-Friendly Chicken Wings 49

   Paleo Kid-Friendly Chicken Fingers...51
   Ranch-Flavored Kid-Friendly Chicken Nuggets....................53

Chapter 4. Paleo Chicken Slow Cooker Recipes..............55
   Spiced Mustard Slow-Cooked Chicken 55
   Southern Living Chicken and Gravy Slow Cooker Paleo Meal
  57
   Long Live Teriyaki Slow Cooked Chicken 59
   Slow Cooked Italian Chicken Cacciatore 60
   Palestine-Inspired Chicken Musakhan...................................62
   Cinnamon-Based Crock Pot Chicken 64
   Korean-Inspired Slow Cooked Kimchi Chicken....................65

Chapter 5. Paleo Chicken Dinner Recipes........................67
   Spiced Garlic and Walnut Stuffed Chicken Breasts 67
   Buffalo Delight Chicken Strips...69
   German-Inspired Chicken Schnitzel......................................71
   Burly Bacon-Wrapped Chicken..73
   Chinese-Inspired Orange Chicken...75
   Indian-Inspired Tandoor Chicken 77
   Almond-Crusted Chicken Breasts 79
   Sunny Day Pistachio Fruit-Stuffed Chicken Breasts............80
   Roasted Sultry Spiced Chicken 82
   Paleo Italian Chicken Parmesan 84
   Grandmother's Ginger Chicken Recipe................................86
   Central American Chicken Adobo...88

Chapter 6. Conclusion...89

About The Author 91

Other Books 92
   One Last Thing..93

Chapter 1. Paleo Chicken Salad Recipes

Thai-Inspired Bok Choy Chicken Salad

Recipe Makes 4 Servings.

Nutritional Breakdown Per Serving: 185 calories, 5 grams carbohydrates, 19 grams protein, 9 grams fat.

Salad Ingredients:

1 ¾ cup chopped grilled chicken

1/3 cup diced jicama

6 grilled and diced bok choy

1/3 cup chopped cilantro

2 ½ diced green onions

1 ¼ tbsp. sesame seeds

Dressing Ingredients:

3 tbsp. coconut cream

¾ tbsp. chopped fresh ginger

1 tsp. sriracha

1 tbsp. soy sauce

¾ tbsp. fish sauce

2 ½ tbsp. lime juice

1 tsp. honey

1 tbsp. sesame oil

Directions:

Begin by mixing the above salad ingredients together in a large mixing bowl. Stir well.

Next, pour all of the dressing ingredients into a food processor or a blender. Blend the ingredients until they're completely assimilated.

Pour the created dressing overtop the salad ingredients, and toss the salad until it's coated.

Allow the salad to chill in the refrigerator for one hour to allow the dressing to assimilate well with the salad ingredients.

Enjoy!

From the Garden Basil Chicken Salad

Recipe Makes 4 Servings.

Nutritional Breakdown Per Serving: 410 calories, 8 grams carbohydrates, 23 grams protein, 33 grams fat.

Ingredients:

2 large, shredded, and pre-cooked skinless chicken breasts

2 small pitted avocadoes

1/3 cup de-stemmed basil leaves

2 ½ tbsp. olive oil

¼ tsp. black pepper

¼ tsp. sea salt

Directions:

Begin by positioning the shredded chicken in your mixing bowl.

Next, add the olive oil, the avocado, the basil, the salt, and the pepper to a food processor. Pulse the ingredients until they're completely smooth.

Add this mixture over the shredded chicken and toss the chicken well to coat it completely. Season the chicken to taste, and allow it to rest in the refrigerator prior to serving.

Chinese-Based Cabbage Chicken Salad

Recipe Makes 4 Servings.

Nutritional Breakdown Per Serving: 207 calories, 13 grams carbohydrates, 19 grams protein, 8 grams fat.

Ingredients:

1 ¾ cup chopped and cooked chicken

4 cups shredded savoy cabbage

1/3 cup julienned scallions

1 cup julienned carrot

1/3 cup chopped cilantro

1/3 cup julienned radishes

1/3 cup chopped mint

Dressing Ingredients:

2 tbsp. sesame oil

2 ¼ tbsp. coconut vinegar

2 ½ tbsp. coconut aminos

1 diced chipotle pepper

juice from ½ lime

1 tsp. honey

3 minced garlic cloves

1 tsp. diced ginger

Directions:

Begin by mixing together the chopped and julienned carrots, cabbage, scallions, and radishes. Add the mint, the cilantro, and the chopped chicken, and toss the salad in a large mixing bowl. Next, position the salad to the side.

To create the vinaigrette, begin by removing the chipotle pepper seeds. Cover the pepper with water and allow it to sit for thirty minutes.

After thirty minutes, add the pepper to the food processor and pulse it for one minute before adding the other ingredients to the processor. Taste the vinaigrette and alter the spices, if you please.

Pour the dressing over the created salad, and toss the salad to coat.

Enjoy!

Mexican-Inspired Chicken Taco Salad

Recipe Makes 3 Servings.

Nutritional Breakdown Per Serving: 328 calories, 14 grams carbohydrates, 24 grams protein, 20 grams fat.

Ingredients:

2 tbsp. taco seasoning (created below)

½ pound shredded chicken

1/3 cup water

1 tbsp. olive oil

1 head shredded lettuce

1 diced tomato

1 diced red onion

1 small, pitted avocado

½ diced green pepper

Directions:

Begin by mixing together the taco seasoning, as followings.

Bring together 1 tsp. garlic powder, 4 tbsp. chili powder, 2 tsp. paprika

1 tsp. onion powder

1 tsp. oregano

¼ tsp. red pepper flakes

3 tsp. salt

Stir the ingredients before taking out the 2 tbsp. of the taco seasoning you require for this recipe. (Note that you can keep the seasoning for a later recipe, if you so choose.)

Next, heat the olive oil in the skillet. Add the chicken to the olive oil to give it a boost of flavor. Pour the water overtop, along with the taco seasoning. Allow the chicken mixture to simmer until the water completely evaporates.

Next, slice and dice all the other ingredients.

Create the salad by assembling together the vegetables, the chicken, etc. Toss the ingredients well, and enjoy!

Indian-Inspired Paleo Curry Chicken Salad

Recipe Makes 2 Servings.

Nutritional Breakdown Per Serving: 437 calories, 36 grams carbohydrates, 33 grams protein, 19 grams fat.

Ingredients:

1 pre-cooked and cooled chicken breast

3 minced garlic cloves

3 diced green onions

2 tbsp. coconut milk

3 tbsp. green curry paste

1/3 cup golden raisins

1/3 cup sundried tomatoes

1/3 cup diced almonds

salt and pepper to taste

Directions:

Begin by shredding the chicken. Place it in a mixing bowl.

Next, add the coconut milk, the onions, the garlic, and the curry paste. Stir well, making sure to coat the chicken.

Next, add the almonds, the raisins, and the sundried tomatoes. Stir well.

Add salt and pepper to taste, and enjoy the salad with greens.

Cilantro and Lime Tangy Chicken Salad

Recipe Makes 5 Servings.

Nutritional Breakdown Per Serving: 391 calories, 10 grams carbohydrates, 42 grams protein, 20 grams fat.

Ingredients:

3 chopped, pre-cooked chicken breasts

1 chopped cabbage

1 sliced cucumber

2 diced avocadoes

juice from 2 limes

6 minced scallions

1 cup chopped cilantro

salt and pepper to taste

Directions:

Begin by mixing together all the above ingredients in a large mixing bowl. Enjoy!

Brussels Sprouts-Based Chicken Salad

Recipe Makes 4 Servings.

Nutritional Breakdown Per Serving: 392 calories, 18 grams carbohydrates, 45 grams protein, 15 grams fat.

Ingredients:

2 chopped pre-cooked chicken breasts

2 cups Brussels sprouts

½ green apple

½ cup diced almonds

½ cup chopped grapes

1 diced white onion

Dressing Ingredients:

1 tbsp. brown mustard

2 tbsp. apple cider vinegar

1 tbsp. honey

1 ½ tbsp. olive oil

½ tsp. sea salt

½ tsp. black pepper

Directions:

Begin by slicing the Brussels sprouts in half. Do this, once more, with the green apple before slicing it into smaller pieces, like matchsticks.

Slice up the grapes, as well, along with the almonds, and the onion.

Chop the chicken, and bring all the ingredients together in a large mixing bowl.

To the side, bring all the dressing ingredients together in a small mixing bowl. Stir the ingredients until they're smooth. Pour this mixture over the Brussels sprouts, and toss the salad well.

Enjoy!

Avocado-Based Paleo Chicken Salad

Recipe Makes 5 Servings.

Nutritional Breakdown Per Serving: 336 calories, 3 grams carbohydrates, 48 grams protein, 12 grams fat.

Ingredients:

3 skinless and boneless chicken breasts, pre-cooked and shredded

1/3 diced onion

1 diced avocado

2 tbsp. lime juice

3 tbsp. cilantro

salt and pepper to taste

Directions:

Bring all the above ingredients together and mix well, making sure to mash the avocado as you go.

Enjoy this very simple recipe.

Paleo Inspiration Apple and Chicken Hash Salad

Recipe Makes 4 Servings.

Nutritional Breakdown Per Serving: 380 calories, 12 grams carbohydrates, 41 grams protein, 18 grams fat.

Ingredients:

2 chicken breasts

1 diced onion

2 tbsp. chopped sage

1 chopped apple

½ tsp. allspice

4 tbsp. coconut oil

1 tbsp. maple syrup

Directions:

Begin by mixing together the sage, the apple, the coconut oil, the onion, and the allspice in a skillet. Cook the ingredients for six minutes, until the onions have turned clear. At this time, add the maple syrup.

Chop up the chicken breasts into tiny, easy-to-eat pieces. Add these to the mixture, and cook them for ten minutes. The chicken should become well done.

Serve this chicken hash with a garden vegetable, and enjoy!

Chapter 2. Paleo Chicken Soup, Chili, and Stew Recipes

Paleo Lazy Day Chicken Veggie Soup

Recipe Makes 8 Servings.

Nutritional Breakdown Per Serving: 140 calories, 12 grams carbohydrates, 13 grams protein, 5 grams fat.

Ingredients:

2 cups shredded pre-cooked chicken

1 sliced leek

1 1/3 cup diced cauliflower

1 diced bell pepper

4 diced carrots

1 diced onion

3 sliced zucchinis

1 cup diced tomatoes

3 sliced celery ribs

3 bay leaves

3 thyme sprigs

7 cups chicken stock

4 minced garlic cloves

2 tbsp. ghee

½ tsp. sea salt

½ tsp. black pepper

Directions:

Begin by melting the ghee in a large stockpot over medium-high heat.

Add the garlic, the onion, the leek, and the pre-cooked chicken and allow them to cook in the fat for approximately six minutes. The onion should be tender.

Next, administer the remaining vegetables, the thyme, the bay leaves, and the chicken broth.

Allow the mixture to boil before turning the heat to medium-low and allowing it to simmer for twenty-two minutes. Stir every few minutes.

Season the mixture with the salt and pepper. Enjoy the soup throughout the winter season!

Kale Creation Chicken Soup

Recipe Makes 8 Servings.

Nutritional Breakdown Per Serving: 215 calories, 7 grams carbohydrates, 28 grams protein, 7 grams fat.

Ingredients:

30 ounces chicken broth

5 sliced carrots

1 entire sliced and diced head of celery

1 chopped head kale

2 diced onion

2 ½ sliced chicken breasts

salt and pepper to taste

Directions:

Begin by bringing every ingredient above, except for the kale, into a large soup pot. Cook the ingredients over medium for approximately forty-five minutes. At this time, the chicken should be fully cooked.

At this time, shred the chicken while it's in the pot.

Add the kale to the soup, and serve the soup warm. Administer salt and pepper to taste. Enjoy!

Paleo Texas-Living Chicken Tortilla Soup

Recipe Makes 8 Servings.

Nutritional Breakdown Per Serving: 215 calories, 11 grams carbohydrates, 29 grams protein, 5 grams fat.

Ingredients:

2 ½ skinless, sliced chicken breasts

1 diced onion

28 ounces canned and diced tomatoes

30 ounces chicken broth

2 ¼ cups diced celery

2 ¼ cups diced carrots

1 diced jalapeno

5 minced garlic cloves

1 chopped bunch cilantro

1 tsp. chili powder

3 tbsp. tomato paste

1 tsp. cumin

2 cups water

1 tbsp. olive oil

salt and pepper to taste

Directions:

Begin by Pouring olive oil and a fourth cup of chicken broth into a large soup pot. Add the garlic, the jalapeno, the onion, the salt, and the pepper to the large soup pot over medium-high heat. Cook the mixture well, until it's soft.

Next, add the remaining ingredients to the large soup pot. After you've added everything, pour enough water into the mixture to allow the soup to reach the very top of the soup pot. Add salt and pepper as you need it.

Next, cover the soup pot and allow the soup to cook for two hours and fifteen minutes.

At this time, shred the chicken with your wooden spoon, pressing it against the side.

Top the mixture with fresh cilantro to serve, if you please, and enjoy!

Thai-Inspired Pumpkin and Chicken Soup

Recipe Makes 5 Servings.

Nutritional Breakdown Per Serving: 273 calories, 10 grams carbohydrates, 13 grams protein, 18 grams fat.

Ingredients:

15 ounces pumpkin puree

4 cups chicken broth

13 ounces coconut milk

½ tsp. sea salt

½ cup cilantro

1 ½ tsp. red curry paste

½ cup diced green onions

½ tsp. Thai fish sauce

15 ounce can of chicken breast

3 minced garlic cloves

Directions:

Begin by mixing all the above ingredients together in a large soup pot. Stir the ingredients well, and allow them to come to a boil.

When the mixture comes to a boil, reduce the heat. Allow it to simmer for twenty minutes.

After twenty minutes, utilize an immersion blender to blend the ingredients a bit, to smooth the soup and create a layered texture.

Enjoy!

Faux Chicken Noodle Soup

Recipe Makes 10 Servings.

Nutritional Breakdown Per Serving: 261 calories, 4 grams carbohydrates, 46 grams protein, 4 grams fat.

Ingredients:

3 ½ pounds chicken breast, diced

3 chopped celery stalks

4 chopped carrots

6 minced garlic cloves

1 diced onion

1 bay leaf

10 cups water

salt and pepper to taste

¼ tsp. white pepper

½ tsp. thyme

2-inch chopped noodles, made from a zucchini, julienned

Directions:

Begin by preheating the oven to 425 degrees Fahrenheit.

Next, slice up the chicken and position the chicken in a large baking dish. Add salt and pepper. Roast the chicken in the oven for twenty-five minutes.

Add the cooked chicken to a large soup pot, and add water. Bring the water to a boil on the stove over medium-high heat. Make sure to boil completely for six minutes.

Next, remove the chicken from the pot. Add the garlic, the onions, the celery, the carrots, and the bay leaf. Reduce the heat to low and allow the ingredients to simmer for forty-five minutes.

At this time, prepare the noodles from the zucchini. Add the zucchini and the chicken back to the pot, and allow the soup to simmer for six minutes.

Enjoy this fake chicken noodle soup!

Chicken Sausage Farm Days Soup

Recipe Makes 8 Servings.

Nutritional Breakdown Per Serving: 271 calories, 17 grams carbohydrates, 22 grams protein, 12 grams fat.

Ingredients:

5 sliced and peeled carrots

2 tbsp. olive oil

1 diced onion

1 ½ pound Italian chicken sausage

6 minced garlic cloves

10 ounces sliced cherry tomatoes

½ tsp. red pepper flakes

½ tsp. black pepper

8 cups chicken broth

10 ounces chopped broccoli

Directions:

Begin by slicing and dicing the onions and the garlic.

Slice the carrots.

Next, remove the chicken sausage from its casing. Trim the broccoli, and slice it up into chunks.

Heat a soup pot over medium-high heat on the stove. After three minutes, add the olive oil into the mixture, and cook the onions and the carrots, stirring every few minutes, for a full ten minutes. The carrots should be tender.

Next, add the garlic and the chicken sausage to the mixture. Cook for seven minutes, continually breaking up the chicken sausage to create chunks.

Next, remove this created mixture from the soup pot and place it to the side. Add the tomatoes to the pot, now, and cook them for four minutes. They should blister. Press each tomato to the side of the pot, at this time, making sure to burst them. Burst all of the tomatoes.

Add the chicken sausage creation back to the tomato pot. Stir well, and cook everything together for two minutes.

Next, pour the broth into the soup pot, and allow the broth to boil. When it begins to boil, add the broccoli and cook for an additional four minutes.

At this time, remove the soup from the heat. Adjust any seasonings as you please, and serve the soup warm.

Enjoy!

Paleo White Winter Wonderland Chicken Chili

Recipe Makes 6 Servings.

Nutritional Breakdown Per Serving: 328 calories, 13 grams carbohydrates, 43 grams protein, 9 grams fat.

Ingredients:

1 ¾ pound chopped chicken breasts

2 diced jalapenos

1 tbsp. olive oil

2 diced onions

1 diced green pepper

1 tsp. coriander

5 minced garlic cloves

5 cups chicken broth

4 tbsp. arrowroot powder

4 tbsp. coconut milk

5 ounces green chiles

Directions:

Begin by chopping up the chicken and the vegetables.

Position a large soup pot over medium-high heat, and cook the onions, the peppers, the oli, the jalapenos, and the garlic in the olive oil for five minutes.

After five minutes, add the salt, the spices, and the chicken. Allow the chicken to sauté for an additional seven minutes.

Pour the broth, the coconut milk, and the green chiles into the soup pot before adding the arrowroot powder slowly. Whisk well.

Allow the soup to come to a boil before lowering the heat to medium-low and allowing it to simmer for twenty-two minutes.

At this time, mash the chicken and create shreds. Serve the chili warm, and enjoy!

Delicious Chipotle Chicken Chili

Recipe Makes 8 Servings.

Nutritional Breakdown Per Serving: 202 calories, 6 grams carbohydrates, 33 grams protein, 3 grams fat.

Ingredients:

2 pounds shredded and cooked chicken

1 cup chicken stock

3 chopped onions

¾ pound chopped tomatoes

3 tbsp. apple cider vinegar

5 minced garlic cloves

3 tbsp. coconut aminos

1 tbsp. chipotle powder

1 tsp. cumin

1 tsp. paprika

1 tsp. cayenne pepper

1 tsp. oregano

1 tsp. black pepper

1 tsp. sea salt

Directions:

Begin by bringing the above ingredients into a large soup pot. Stir the ingredients well.

Allow the mixture to come to a boil before covering the pot. Reduce the heat to low and allow it to simmer for four hours.

Enjoy!

Mexican-Inspired Chicken Chili

Recipe Makes 4 Servings.

Nutritional Breakdown Per Serving: 407 calories, 24 grams carbohydrates, 45 grams protein, 14 grams fat.

Ingredients:

1 ¼ pound skinless and boneless chicken breasts

1 diced onion

4 minced bell peppers

2 ¼ cup salsa

1 diced jalapeno pepper

2 cups water

3 minced garlic cloves

1 tsp. chili powder

1 tsp. cumin

1 diced avocado

salt and pepper to taste

Directions:

Begin by bringing together the garlic, the salsa, the chicken breasts, the cumin, the water, the onion, the chili powder, the salt, and the pepper into a large soup pot. Stir well before covering the soup pot and allowing it to simmer on low for three hours.

Next, remove the chicken from the soup pot and shred it before returning it back to the soup pot.

At this time, saute the jalapeno and the bell peppers in a skillet with a bit of olive oil for five minutes. Add these to the soup pot. Stir well, and cover once more.

Allow the chili to continue to simmer for twenty-five minutes.

Add the avocado to the top of the chili prior to serving, and enjoy!

Paleo Faux-Cream Southern Living Chicken Stew

Recipe Makes 10 Servings.

Nutritional Breakdown Per Serving: 370 calories, 9 grams carbohydrates, 49 grams protein, 14 grams fat.

Ingredients:

3 ½ pound chicken

1/3 cup ghee

3 minced garlic cloves

3 diced onions

2 cups chicken broth

1/3 cup almond flour

3 diced carrots

5 sliced mushrooms

1 cup green peas, either fresh or frozen

3 sliced green onions

1/3 cup coconut milk

salt and pepper to taste

Directions:

Begin by slicing and dicing the chicken.

To the side, melt the ghee in a saucepan and add the chicken. Cook the chicken until it's browned on all sides. When it's done, place it to the side.

Next, add the onions to the saucepan. Cook the onion in the ghee. After they've begun to brown, add the garlic. Cook for an additional six minutes.

At this time, add the almond flour to the onion and the garlic, and stir well. Pour the chicken broth into the mixture. Stir well, administering more broth if you feel the stew is too thick.

Next, add the chicken and the vegetables to the stew. Season the stew with any salt and pepper.

When the stew comes to a simmer, cook the stew on low. Maintain the simmer. Cover the stew and allow it to cook for thirty-five minutes.

Next, add the coconut milk, the peas, and the green onions, and cook for an additional two minutes.

Enjoy!

Mediterranean Chicken Stew

Recipe Makes 4 Servings.

Nutritional Breakdown Per Serving: 436 calories, 13 grams carbohydrates, 62 grams protein, 14 grams fat.

Ingredients:

1 ¾ pounds chopped chicken

28 ounces chopped tomatoes

8 minced garlic cloves

30 olives

2 cups chicken broth

2 tbsp. minced basil

2 tbsp. minced rosemary

2 tbsp. minced parsley

1 tbsp. ghee

salt and pepper to taste

Directions:

Begin by preheating the oven to 325 degrees Fahrenheit.

Next, salt and pepper each piece of chicken. Melt the ghee in an oven and stovetop-safe dish, and then brown each of the chicken pieces for three minutes. Add the garlic to the dish, as well, along with the olives, the tomatoes, the rosemary, the chicken broth, and the thyme. Cover the dish and position it in the preheated oven for sixty minutes.

Net, add the parsley and the basil to the dish and position the dish back in the oven, this time without a cover, for forty minutes.

Enjoy!

African-Inspired Chicken Stew

Recipe Makes 4 Servings.

Nutritional Breakdown Per Serving: 470 calories, 15 grams carbohydrates, 47 grams protein, 24 grams fat.

Ingredients:

1 tbsp. coconut oil

1 ¼ pound skinless chicken breasts

1 diced onion

salt and pepper to taste

4 minced garlic cloves

1-inch diced piece ginger

1 bay leaf

½ tbsp. coriander

1/3 cup water

1 ¼ cup crushed tomatoes

1/3 cup sunflower butter

¼ tsp. vanilla

Directions:

Begin by salting and peppering the chicken well.

Heat a large Dutch oven over medium-high for approximately four minutes. Add the coconut oil to the bottom and allow it to melt.

Next, place the chicken at the bottom and brown the chicken on each of its sides. After the chicken browns, place it to the side.

Next, cook the ginger and the onions in the pot until they're soft. This should take about eight minutes. Next, add the coriander, the garlic, and the bay leaf. Cook for approximately one minute before adding the water and the tomatoes. Stir well.

Place the chicken inside the created sauce.

Boost the heat to high to allow it to boil. When it begins to boil, reduce the heat to medium-low and cook for twenty-five minutes, covered.

Afterwards, remove the chicken from the pot. Break it up.

Next, add the sunflower butter and the vanilla to the soup pot. Stir well. Add the chicken back to the stew and cover, allowing it to cook for an additional six minutes.

Serve the stew warm, and enjoy.

Chapter 3. Paleo Chicken Just-for-Kids Recipes

Thai-Inspired Kid-Friendly Paleo Chicken Pizza

Recipe Makes 4 Servings.

Nutritional Breakdown Per Serving: 355 calories, 32 grams carbohydrates, 17 grams protein, 19 grams fat.

Paleo Pizza Crust Ingredients:

2 ¼ cups almond flour

½ tsp. sea salt

½ tsp. garlic powder

2 eggs

½ tsp. baking soda

1 tbsp. olive oil

Pizza Ingredients:

1 minced garlic cloves

2 tbsp. apple cider vinegar

1 de-seeded red chili

1/3 cup honey

1/3 cup water

½ tsp. arrowroot starch

1 egg yolk

¾ cup shredded and pre-cooked chicken

1 diced red onion

½ diced red pepper

1/3 diced zucchini

4 tbsp. coconut milk

Directions:

Begin by preheating the oven to 425 degrees.

To the side, begin by creating the paleo pizza crust. Stir together the almond flour, the salt, the garlic powder, the eggs, the soda, and the olive oil. You can use a food processor if you want it to be really smooth. Then, spread the paleo pizza crust, and bake it for eight minutes in the preheated oven.

At this time, prepare the rest of the pizza.

Place the red chili, the vinegar, the garlic, and the salt together in a food processor, and pulse the ingredients until they're chopped.

Pour this created mixture into a saucepan, and add the arrowroot starch and just one tbsp. of the water. Add the honey, and bring the mixture to a simmer, stirring all the time.

After the mixture begins to thicken, remove it from the heat and place it to the side.

At this time, spread the created sauce overtop the pizza crust. Add the vegetables overtop the chili sauce, followed by the chicken.

Next, to the side, stir together the egg yolk and the coconut milk to the side. Pour this mixture over the toppings.

Bake the pizza for ten minutes, until the crust is golden.

Enjoy the pizza warm.

Finger Lickin' Good Kid-Friendly Chicken Wings

Recipe Makes 10 Servings.

Nutritional Breakdown Per Serving: 279 calories, 10 grams carbohydrates, 36 grams protein, 9 grams fat.

Ingredients:

2 ¾ pound separated chicken wings

1/3 cup lemon juice

1/3 cup honey

1/3 cup water

2 tbsp. tamari soy sauce

2 tsp. garlic powder

2 ½ tbsp. apple cider vinegar

1 tsp. ground ginger

Directions:

Begin by bringing the lemon juice, the honey, the soy sauce, the water, the garlic, the vinegar, and the ginger together in a saucepan. Heat it over medium-high, stirring a bit. When it begins to simmer, turn the heat to low and allow it to simmer for five minutes before allowing it to cool.

Pour this mixture over the chicken wings. Allow the chicken to marinate in the refrigerator for three hours.

Next, preheat the oven to 400 degrees Fahrenheit. Bake the chicken wings for sixty minutes in the preheated oven, making sure to turn them over after thirty minutes.

Enjoy!

Paleo Kid-Friendly Chicken Fingers

Recipe Makes 4 Servings.

Nutritional Breakdown Per Serving: 314 calories, 6 grams carbohydrates, 37 grams protein, 15 grams fat.

Ingredients:

1 pound no-bone, no-skin chicken, sliced into chicken fingers

1 cup shredded coconut

1 ¼ cup almond flour

1 tsp. paprika

1 egg

½ tsp. garlic powder

1 tsp. onion powder

½ tsp. cumin

Directions:

Begin by preheating the oven to 375 degrees Fahrenheit.

Next, lay out the chicken strips on a piece of parchment paper. Season both sides of the chicken with the paprika, the garlic, the cumin, and the onion powder.

To the side, whisk up the egg. In another bowl, stir together the coconut and the almond flour.

Dip the chicken strips first in the egg, then in the flour mixture. Coat each of them well.

Place the chicken strips on a baking sheet, and bake them for twenty minutes.

Enjoy!

Ranch-Flavored Kid-Friendly Chicken Nuggets

Recipe Makes 5 Servings.

Nutritional Breakdown Per Serving: 279 calories, 4 grams carbohydrates, 30 grams protein, 15 grams fat.

Ingredients:

1 pound boneless, skinless, bite-sized chicken pieces

½ tsp. dried dill

½ tbsp. parsley

½ tsp. onion powder

½ tsp. garlic powder

½ cup coconut milk

½ tsp. basil

1 egg

2 ¼ cup almond flour

Directions:

Begin by preheating the oven to 375 degrees Fahrenheit.

To the side, mix together the dill, the parsley, the onion powder, the garlic powder, the pepper, the basil, the egg, and the coconut milk in a small bowl. Pour this fake ranch into a large storage bag.

Add the pieces of chicken to the bag, as well, and shake the sealed bag well to coat the chicken.

Add the almond flour to the bag and continue to shake to give it a nice coating.

Position the chicken nuggets on a baking sheet and bake them for twenty minutes. They should be golden brown.

Enjoy!

Chapter 4. Paleo Chicken Slow Cooker Recipes

Spiced Mustard Slow-Cooked Chicken

Recipe Makes 4 Servings.

Nutritional Breakdown Per Serving: 297 calories, 12 grams carbohydrates, 41 grams protein, 8 grams fat.

Ingredients:

2 medium-sized chicken breasts

1 tsp. garlic powder

1 tbsp. olive oil

½ cup chicken broth

2 ½ tbsp. honey

2 tbsp. Dijon mustard

3 minced garlic cloves

2 tbsp. Stone-ground mustard

salt and pepper to taste

Directions:

Begin by stirring together all the ingredients—except for the chicken—in a bowl.

Position the chicken in the base of the slow cooker, and pour the created sauce overtop.

Cover the slow cooker, and allow the chicken to cook for three hours on LOW.

At this time, remove the chicken from the slow cooker. Pour the created sauce into a saucepan, and allow it to simmer for fifteen minutes.

Serve the chicken warm with the created sauce, and enjoy.

Southern Living Chicken and Gravy Slow Cooker Paleo Meal

Recipe Makes 12 Servings.

Nutritional Breakdown Per Serving: 276 calories, 3 grams carbohydrates, 44 grams protein, 7 grams fat.

Ingredients:

4 pounds whole chicken

7 minced garlic cloves

3 tbsp. ghee

3 diced onions

1/3 cup chicken stock

1 tsp. tomato paste

1/3 cup white wine

1 tsp. basil

1 tsp. oregano

½ tsp. sea salt

½ tsp. black pepper

Directions:

Begin by slicing and dicing the vegetables.

Melt the ghee in a skillet over medium, and sauté the garlic and the onion for approximately five minutes. Add the tomato paste at this time, and cook for an additional ten minutes. Add salt and pepper.

Next, pour this mixture into your slow cooker.

Season the chicken with the basil, the oregano, the salt, and the pepper, and then place the chicken with its breast down in the slow cooker. Add the cover overtop, and allow the chicken to cook for six hours on LOW.

After it finishes cooking, remove the chicken from the slow cooker and allow it to cool for twenty-five minutes.

At this time, blend the remaining vegetables and fat in the bottom of the slow cooker with the immersion blender. This is your gravy.

Next, rip up the chicken and serve the chicken with the created gravy.

Enjoy!

Long Live Teriyaki Slow Cooked Chicken

Recipe Makes 5 Servings.

Nutritional Breakdown Per Serving: 330 calories, 5 grams carbohydrates, 59 grams protein, 5 grams fat.

Ingredients:

2 ¼ pound chicken thighs

1 tbsp. honey

1/3 cup coconut aminos

3 minced garlic cloves

1 ½ tbsp. grated ginger

salt and pepper to taste

Directions:

Position the chicken in the slow cooker.

To the side, mix together the honey, the coconut aminos, the garlic cloves, and the ginger.

Pour this created sauce over the chicken. Cook the chicken on LOW for five hours.

Next, remove the chicken from the slow cooker, salt and pepper it to taste, and enjoy!

Slow Cooked Italian Chicken Cacciatore

Recipe Makes 8 Servings.

Nutritional Breakdown Per Serving: 313 calories, 21 grams carbohydrates, 38 grams protein, 9 grams fat.

Ingredients:

2 pounds chicken thighs

2 diced onions

5 minced garlic cloves

2 diced zucchinis

12 ounces tomato paste

28 ounces diced tomatoes

1 tsp. chopped basil

14 ounces artichoke hearts

salt and pepper to taste

Directions:

Begin by lining the bottom of the slow cooker with zucchini and onion. Position the chicken overtop the vegetables, and add garlic.

Next, follow the chicken with the paste and the tomatoes. Add the artichokes overtop.

Spread the basil, the pepper, and the salt overtop. Place the lid over the slow cooker, and cook the chicken on LOW for eight hours.

Enjoy with spaghetti squash.

Palestine-Inspired Chicken Musakhan

Recipe Makes 8 Servings.

Nutritional Breakdown Per Serving: 375 calories, 5 grams carbohydrates, 42 grams protein, 19 grams fat.

Ingredients:

2 ½ pounds skinless chicken thighs

2 tbsp. olive oil

3 diced onions

½ ounce ground sumac

½ tsp. ground cloves

1 tsp. cinnamon

½ tsp. allspice

½ cup pine nuts

salt and pepper to taste

Directions:

Begin by mixing together the olive oil, the onions, the sumac, the allspice, the cinnamon, and the cloves in a microwave-safe bowl. Microwave the mixture for three minutes. Stir well, and microwave for an additional two minutes.

Next, pour this mixture into the slow cooker.

Add the chicken to the slow cooker, and salt and pepper it well. Position it well in the onion mixture.

Cook the chicken on LOW for six hours.

Just before serving, add the pine nuts and a small dash of olive oil to a skillet and sauté them until they're browned.

Serve the chicken and the vegetables warm, topped with pine nuts.

Enjoy!

Cinnamon-Based Crock Pot Chicken

Recipe Makes 6 Servings.

Nutritional Breakdown Per Serving: 364 calories, 7 grams carbohydrates, 51 grams protein, 13 grams fat.

Ingredients:

2 ¼ pound chicken breasts

1 diced onion

3 sliced bell peppers

5 minced garlic cloves

3 tsp. cinnamon

1 ¼ cup chicken broth

½ tsp. nutmeg

Directions:

Begin by mixing all the above ingredients well in a slow cooker. Cook the chicken on LOW for six hours before serving warm.

Enjoy!

Korean-Inspired Slow Cooked Kimchi Chicken

Recipe Makes 6 Servings.

Nutritional Breakdown Per Serving: 241 calories, 3 grams carbohydrates, 38 grams protein, 7 grams fat.

Ingredients:

2 ¼ pound skinless, boneless chicken breasts

1 cup chicken broth

5 diced scallions

7 minced garlic cloves

2 tsp. date sugar

1 tbsp. soy sauce

1 tsp. grated ginger

1 tsp. sesame oil

2 cups cabbage kimchi

Directions:

Begin by mixing all of the ingredients except for the chicken, the scallions, and the kimchi in the slow cooker.

Next, add the chicken to the slow cooker, wedging it inside the other ingredients, making sure to cover it well with the mixture.

Cover the slow cooker and allow the chicken to cook for five hours on LOW.

When you wish to serve the chicken, place the heat to high. Add the kimchi to the slow cooker and cook the kimchi for twenty minutes, mixed in with everything else.

Serve the chicken kimchi with scallion greens overtop.

Enjoy!

Chapter 5. Paleo Chicken Dinner Recipes

Spiced Garlic and Walnut Stuffed Chicken Breasts

Recipe Makes 4 Servings.

Nutritional Breakdown Per Serving: 290 calories, 3 grams carbohydrates, 21 grams protein, 22 grams fat.

Ingredients:

2 chicken breasts

4 ounces basil leaves

½ cup diced walnuts

1 tsp. dried rosemary

2 ½ tbsp. olive oil

3 minced garlic cloves

salt and pepper to taste

Directions:

Preheat the oven to 375 degrees Fahrenheit.

Begin by bringing together the basil, the oil, the walnuts, and the garlic in a food processor. Create a paste, a pesto.

Next, slit the side of each chicken breast and "open" them. Cover them with wrap and beat at them to flatten them. You can use a meat mallet or another heavy object.

Next, position one tbsp. of the pesto mixture into the center of each chicken breast. Roll the chicken breasts closed.

Season the chicken breasts with salt, pepper, and rosemary, and then bake the chicken for thirty-five minutes.

Enjoy!

Buffalo Delight Chicken Strips

Recipe Makes 6 Servings.

Nutritional Breakdown Per Serving: 205 calories, 2 grams carbohydrates, 34 grams protein, 6 grams fat.

Ingredients:

2 pounds skinless, boneless chicken breasts

4 tbsp. cayenne pepper

1/3 cup apple cider vinegar

1/3 cup water

½ tsp. garlic powder

½ tsp. cumin

½ tsp. chili powder

Directions:

Begin by slicing the chicken into strips.

Position the chicken strips in a ziplock baggie. Add the water, the vinegar, and the cayenne pepper to the bag. Move the ingredients around well, distributing the spices. Seal the bag, next, and position it in the refrigerator for forty minutes.

At this time, preheat the oven to 350 degrees Fahrenheit.

Next, position each of the chicken pieces onto a baking sheet, Add the seasoning overtop the chicken, on both sides.

Bake the chicken breasts for twenty minutes, and enjoy.

German-Inspired Chicken Schnitzel

Recipe Makes 4 Servings.

Nutritional Breakdown Per Serving: 475 calories, 12 grams carbohydrates, 39 grams protein, 30 grams fat.

Ingredients:

4 chicken breasts

3 eggs

2 cups arrowroot powder

3 ½ cups shredded coconut

ghee

Directions:

Begin by slicing and dicing each of the chicken breasts into tenderloin-sized pieces.

Position the arrowroot powder in a bowl. Place the cracked egg in a separate bowl. Add the coconut to the last bowl. Make sure you whisk the egg.

Next, dip the chicken pieces into first the arrowroot powder, then the egg, then the coconut. Position the chicken to the side.

At this time, heat the ghee in a fry pan. Fry the chicken pieces on both sides, until they're golden brown.

Serve warm, and enjoy!

Burly Bacon-Wrapped Chicken

Recipe Makes 4 Servings.

Nutritional Breakdown Per Serving: 444 calories, 25 grams carbohydrates, 35 grams protein, 24 grams fat.

Ingredients:

2 boneless, skinless chicken breasts

8 slices no-sugar bacon

½ tsp. sea salt

4 chopped artichoke hearts

40 grams chopped sundried tomatoes

1/3 cup chopped water chestnuts

2 minced garlic cloves

1/3 cup pine nuts

½ tsp. black pepper

1 tsp. chopped rosemary

½ tsp. paprika

Directions:

Begin by creating the stuffing by mixing together all but the chicken, the bacon, and the initial salt in a medium-sized mixing bowl. Set the stuffing to the side.

Next, preheat the oven to 375 degrees Fahrenheit.

Butterfly the chicken breasts by slicing the side of the chicken breasts. Open the chicken breasts like a book, and then pound them to create a slight thickness—about half an inch.

Position the chicken breasts on the cutting board and salt them. Add half of the created stuffing to the chicken breasts. Spread it evenly, and do not go near the edges.

Roll up the chicken breasts well, and then wrap the chicken breasts with bacon slices.

Position the wrapped chicken breasts in a baking dish. Cover them with aluminum foil, and bake them for forty minutes.

At this time, remove the foil and drain the baking dish of any juices.

Next, bake the chicken, uncovered this time, for an additional twenty minutes. This will crisp up the bacon.

Remove the chicken from the oven and allow the chicken to cool for ten minutes prior to serving. Enjoy!

CHINESE-INSPIRED ORANGE CHICKEN

Recipe Makes 4 Servings.

Nutritional Breakdown Per Serving: 253 calories, 21 grams carbohydrates, 27 grams protein, 6 grams fat.

Ingredients:

3 chicken breasts

1/3 cup soy sauce

2 ½ cups concentrate, frozen orange juice, no water

1 ½ tbsp. garlic powder

1 tsp. basil

1 tsp. thyme

Directions:

Begin by remove the skin from the chicken. Position the chicken breasts in a ziplock bag, and set them to the side.

Next, mix together the marinade: the orange juice, the soy sauce, and the garlic powder. Do not add water. Afterwards, pour this created marinade over the chicken in the plastic bag. Allow the chicken to marinate in the refrigerator for ten hours.

Next, preheat the oven for 450 degrees Fahrenheit.

Remove all the excess orange marinade from the chicken and throw it away. Rub at the chicken with the spices.

Bake the chicken for twenty-five minutes, until it's orange-brown. Remove the chicken, and enjoy warm.

Indian-Inspired Tandoor Chicken

Recipe Makes 6 Servings.

Nutritional Breakdown Per Serving: 379 calories, 3 grams carbohydrates, 50 grams protein, 17 grams fat.

Ingredients:

½ cup coconut cream

1 tbsp. minced ginger

3 minced garlic cloves

juice from 1 lemon

2 tsp. garam masala

1 tbsp. paprika

1 tsp. cayenne

1 tsp. coriander

2 ¼ pound skinless chicken breasts

skewers

Directions:

Begin by bringing the coconut cream, the ginger, the garlic, the lemon, the garam masala, the paprika, the cayenne, and the coriander together in a medium-sized mixing bowl. Set the mixture to the side.

Next, slice and dice the chicken breasts to create small cubes. Add these into the created mixture, coating them well. Cover the bowl with aluminum foil and allow the mixture to refrigerate for a whole day.

Next, soak each of the skewers in water for a half hour.

Place the chicken on each skewer, filling the skewers.

Grill the chicken on both sides for approximately eight to ten minutes. Enjoy warm!

Almond-Crusted Chicken Breasts

Recipe Makes 8 Servings.

Nutritional Breakdown Per Serving: 332 calories, 4 grams carbohydrates, 41 grams protein, 16 grams fat.

Ingredients:

2 ¼ pound chicken breasts

2 tbsp. chili powder

3 eggs

¾ cup almond meal

1 tbsp. Italian seasoning

1 tsp. cayenne

¾ tbsp. garlic powder

salt and pepper to taste

Directions:

Begin by preheating the oven to 400 degrees Fahrenheit.

Next, mix together the dry ingredients on a large dinner plate.

To the side, beat the eggs in a small bowl.

First, dip each of the chicken breasts in the egg. Then, stir the breasts in the dry ingredients to evenly coat them.

Place the chicken breasts on the baking dish and bake them for thirteen minutes on each side. Serve warm, and enjoy.

Sunny Day Pistachio Fruit-Stuffed Chicken Breasts

Recipe Makes 10 Servings.

Nutritional Breakdown Per Serving: 252 calories, 30 grams carbohydrates, 22 grams protein, 4 grams fat.

Ingredients:

5 skinless, boneless chicken breasts

10 ounces concentrated, frozen orange and pineapple juice, well thawed

1 tsp. ground ginger

¼ cup white wine

¼ chopped pineapple

1/3 chopped orange

½ chopped papaya

1/3 cup chopped pistachios

Directions:

Begin by mixing the juice, the ginger, and the wine together in a medium-sized bowl. Set the bowl to the side.

Next, cleanse the chicken breasts, and then butterfly them, opening them like a book. Flatten the chicken breasts with a meat mallet or with a rolling pin to create a fourth of an inch thickness.

Next, place the pounded chicken in the marinade, and store the chicken in the refrigerator, covered, for ten hours.

After ten hours, preheat the oven to 400 degrees Fahrenheit.

Mix together the pineapple, the oranges, the papaya, and the pistachios in a small bowl. Bring this stuffing into the inside of the pounded chicken breasts, and then roll the chicken breasts closed. Secure them with toothpicks.

Bake the chicken breasts for forty-five minutes. Afterwards, serve the chicken warm, and enjoy!

Roasted Sultry Spiced Chicken

Recipe Makes 6 Servings.

Nutritional Breakdown Per Serving: 442 calories, 1 gram carbohydrate, 54 grams protein, 21 grams fat.

Ingredients:

2 ½ pounds chicken breasts

1 tsp. paprika

½ tsp. oregano

3 tbsp. olive oil

½ tsp. sea salt

½ tsp. cumin

½ tsp. black pepper

2 sliced lemons

parsley

Directions:

Begin by preheating the oven to 400 degrees Fahrenheit.

To the side, mix together the pepper, the salt, the oregano, the paprika, the olive oil, and the cumin.

Slice the lemons.

Position the chicken breasts in a baking dish, and coat them with the spices. Add the lemon slices overtop.

Bake the chicken without a cover for fifty minutes in the preheated oven. Serve the chicken with parsley overtop, and enjoy.

Paleo Italian Chicken Parmesan

Recipe Makes 10 Servings.

Nutritional Breakdown Per Serving: 445 calories, 15 grams carbohydrates, 38 grams protein, 33 grams fat.

Ingredients:

2 ½ pounds skinless and boneless chicken breasts

½ cup arrowroot powder

½ cup coconut flour

4 eggs

½ tsp. garlic powder

½ tsp. basil

½ tsp. sea salt

24 ounces red pasta sauce

2 cups coconut oil

Directions:

Begin by adding 2 cups of coconut oil into a skillet. Melt it on medium-high.

Next, butterfly the chicken breasts by slicing them on the side and then pounding them to create a half-inch thickness.

To the side, whisk the eggs together in a small bowl.

In a separate dish, stir together the spices, the coconut flour, and the arrowroot powder.

Next, dip the chicken first into the egg, then into the arrowroot powder mixture. Coat the chicken well.

Place the chicken on the coconut oil and cook them until they brown. This should be about five minutes on each side.

To the side, heat the pasta sauce until it's hot.

Next, after the chicken has cooked, place the chicken in a baking dish. Top the chicken with pasta sauce, and broil the chicken for just four minutes.

Serve the chicken Parmesan warm, and enjoy!

Grandmother's Ginger Chicken Recipe

Recipe Makes 4 Servings.

Nutritional Breakdown Per Serving: 366 calories, 3 grams carbohydrates, 49 grams protein, 16 grams fat.

Ingredients:

1-inch sliced ginger

1 ½ pound chicken legs

1 tsp. sea salt

1 tsp. black pepper

1 diced red onion

1 diced green onion

1 tbsp. coconut oil

Directions:

Begin by bringing the ginger, the onion, and the coconut oil together in a skillet. Cook them together for four minutes over medium heat.

At this time, add the chicken leg to the skillet. Season the chicken well, and cover the skillet.

Reduce the stovetop temperature to low, and allow the chicken to cook for forty minutes.

At this time, the chicken leg will have released its water to create a ginger sauce.

Garnish the chicken with the green onions, and serve warm. Enjoy.

Central American Chicken Adobo

Recipe Makes 4 Servings.

Nutritional Breakdown Per Serving: 369 calories, 3 grams carbohydrates, 65 grams protein, 6 grams fat.

Ingredients:

2 pounds chicken

7 minced garlic cloves

1 cup water

1/3 cup tamari

1/3 cup apple cider vinegar

20 pcs. Peppercorns

Directions:

Begin by heating the chicken, the water, the garlic, the peppercorn, the apple cider vinegar, and the black pepper in a medium-sized pan.

After the water begins to boil, place the heat on LOW and allow the chicken to simmer for sixty minutes.

At this time, serve the chicken adobo, and enjoy.

Chapter 6. Conclusion

These Paleo diet chicken recipes lend you a perfect path toward bettering your life. They bring you essential proteins, fats, and a minimal number of carbohydrates to help you lose weight, age gracefully, and refute serious diseases, like depression, anxiety, obesity, and heart disease.

Because chicken is the main ingredient in each of the recipes, you are able to:

1. Build healthy muscles with the bountiful proteins, each with an appropriate number of amino acids for healthy muscle growth.
2. Lose weight easily with the high level of protein versus the low number of carbohydrates.
3. Boost your heart health by decreasing your body's level of bad amino acid, homocysteine.
4. Build healthy bones with the mineral, phosphorous, which further supports bone, kidney, liver, and nervous system functionality.
5. Rev your metabolism with chicken's selenium, a mineral that boosts your thyroid and your immune functionality.
6. And so much more.

This book offers a solution to the current world's problems with obesity, heart disease, cancers, and depressions. Armed with healthful, nutrient-rich recipes, you can create a better world for your mind and your body.

Too often, we turn toward medicines, toward doctors for things we can fix with the spices, the good meats, and the vegetables in our kitchens at home.

Remember, as Hippocrates said: "Let thy food be thy medicine, and thy medicine be thy food."

Good luck on your journey to greater health.

About The Author

Since Paolo Ferrari moved to the USA from Italy, he was 16 years old, he knew he wanted to be a chef. Growing up, he was incredibly intrigued by cooking and by how he could make people happy through food, so he read as many cook books as he could get his hands on, and took as many cooking courses as possible.

When he was still attending high school, Paolo began working at a steakhouse. He has remained a member of the team since then, only leaving long enough to earn a degree in culinary arts from The Florida Culinary Institute in Palm Beach, FL in 2010.

Paolo is now a paleo lifestyle expert on his own time. He is passionate about the diet and believes everyone should give it a shot.

OTHER BOOKS

Ultimate Guide to the Paleo Diet: *Paleo Diet for Beginners*

ONE LAST THING...

If you enjoyed this book or found it useful I'd be very grateful if you'd post a short review on Amazon. Your support really does make a difference and I read all the reviews personally so I can get your feedback and make this book even better.

Thanks again for your support!

Printed in Great Britain
by Amazon